1986

Henri Matisse

ACKNOWLEDGMENTS

Illustrations: Rory Kee
Tom Stimpson (pp. 8–9)
Design: Judith Escreet
Picture research: Linda Proud

Picture Credits
Cover, p. 6 Cameraphoto, Venice; pp. 8, 9, 44
Photo Hélène Adant; p. 34 (bottom) Photo Walter
Carne, Paris Match; p. 35 Collection Musées de
France; p. 43 Collezione d'Arte Religiosa
Moderna, Vatican Museums (Photo Scala); p. 16
Det Danske Kunstindustrimuseum, Copenhagen;
p. 34 (top) Courtesy of Detroit Institute of Arts
(gift of John S. Newberry); p. 25 Ikeda Museum
of 20th Century Art, Itoh, Japan; pp. 16–17
Kuntsmuseum, Basle (Photo Hans Hinz); pp. 22,
23 Mobilier National, on loan to Musée National
d'Arte Moderne; p. 42 Musée Matisse, Nice;
pp. 20, 21 Musée National d'Art Moderne, Paris;
p. 28 Museum of Modern Art, New York (gift of
the artist); pp. 38–39 Museum of Modern Art,
New York (Mrs. Bernard F. Gimbel Fund);
pp. 36–37 Stedelijk Museum, Amsterdam; p. 33
Tate Gallery, London; pp. 10, 11, 26, 27, 30 from
private collections

Special thanks to Söeur Paul, Chapelle Matisse;
Maria-Gaetana Matisse; Patrick Ducournau, Musée
Matisse; Jack Cowart, Saint Louis Art Museum

Quotes in translation from *Henri Matisse:
Ecrits et propos sur l'art*, ed. Dominique Fourcade
(Paris: Hermann, 1972)

First published in 1983 by Walker Books Ltd,
17–19 Hanway House, Hanway Place,
London W1P 9DL

Design and illustrations copyright © 1983
Walker Books Ltd

Text copyright © 1983 Nelly Munthe

First printed 1983   Printed in Italy   AHS

Library of Congress Cataloging in Publication Data

Munthe, Nelly.
  Meet Matisse.

  Summary: An introduction to the cut-outs of Henri
Matisse, who concentrated on this technique of artistic
expression in his final years. Instructions are
included for several of Matisse's artistic techniques.
  1. Matisse, Henri, 1869–1954—Juvenile literature.
2. Artists—France—Biography—Juvenile literature.
3. Cut-outs (Decorative arts)—Technique—Juvenile
literature. [1. Matisse, Henri, 1869–1954. 2. Artists.
3. Cut-outs (Decorative arts)—Technique. 4. Art—
Technique] I. Title.
NK8553.5.M38M86 1983   709'.2'4 [92]   83–9905
ISBN 0-316-58960-8

THE CUTOUTS

MEET

Matisse

Written by Nelly Munthe

LITTLE, BROWN AND COMPANY
BOSTON   TORONTO

Matisse "drawing" with scissors

Henri Matisse was a French artist who lived between 1869 and 1954. His life had been dedicated to painting in oils. All his subjects—women, flowers, landscapes, still life compositions—show his fascination with bright colors and their subtle relationships. When he was an old man, ill and confined to his bed or to a wheelchair, he had time at last to think about what he had tried to do through his painting. He wrote: "My terrible operation has made a philosopher of me . . . it seems to me now that I am in a second life." He felt free and detached.

Matisse was weak, his strength diminished—the time had come for him to simplify his way of seeing things and his way of doing things. Instead of taking a pen or a paintbrush, he took a pair of scissors.

For Matisse, the cutouts were the last stage on a road that had taken him his lifetime. This book explores that last part of his life.

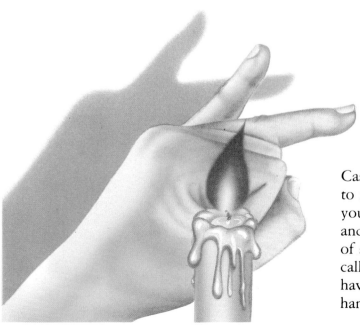

Casting shadows is one way to make cutouts. Try it yourself, arranging your hand and fingers to cast the shadow of a rabbit, perhaps. You can call this a cutout because you have cut out the light with a handful of shade.

Of course, cutouts had been done before. Maybe the first cutout was made when someone put his or her hand in front of a candle to cast a shadow against a white wall. Artists began to use this way of seeing things to make pictures or images that would last. They cut out shapes, put them in front of a light, against a screen, made them move, and invented shadow puppets. Later they cut out shapes, glued them to a background, and made silhouettes. The Chinese and Japanese made beautiful silhouettes of dragons, birds, butterflies, and flowers.

In Europe in the eighteenth century, it became fashionable to make silhouettes of people, and these were usually in black. Black was used to create the greatest possible contrast with the white background.

A silhouette is made when you trace the outline of a shadow and then cut it out.

In Indonesia, shadow puppets of parchment are used to tell stories and legends.

Modern Chinese cutouts like this elaborate mask are glued to walls and windows.

The spreading, cascading cheese plant in Matisse's studio

Matisse's cutouts are very special. They are not black and white. The shapes he cut out are not the shadows of a real object; they do not "photograph" the object in the sense that the silhouettes and shadow puppets do. They are the work of a painter, of an artist. The leaves he cut out, for instance, the colors he chose, came from a special world—his world. He has not conveyed a piece of information to us, but his feeling. Matisse wrote: "The cutout is what I have found to be the simplest and most direct way of expressing myself."

Imagine Matisse in his bright studio in Nice, confined to his wheelchair. His assistants are bustling around him. "I am like a traveler," he said. "My suitcases are packed and I am waiting for the train, but I do not know when it leaves." Matisse felt that if he was to realize his ideas, with so little time and strength left, he had to find a new way of working. The cutout technique required less physical strength than the oil paintings of his earlier years.

The preparatory work was left to his assistants. He chose the papers and the colors, and they painted the large sheets with opaque watercolors called gouache. The sheets were then hung up all around the walls to dry.

Now Matisse's work began. What could he see? The light streaming through the large windows, which vibrated over his colored sheets; a few sculptures that he loved, wall hangings from Morocco, a few tiles and plants. The iridescent shapes of the leaves started to play in his mind. He took his scissors, cut straight into a color, and carved out his shape like a sculptor.

Matisse, surrounded by cutaway
shapes carved from his memory

9

Black Leaf on Red Background 1952
size 50 cm x 40 cm

Matisse had a catalogue of images in his head. At seventy-one he had watched, felt, and drawn the objects around him so often that they now *belonged* to him. He was able to represent them with his own signs and shapes. He had his own language of colors and forms. With his experience as a painter he could now communicate his feelings to us—more, he had the new tools to make us understand what touched him.

Matisse first made lots of pictures of a single leaf on different-colored backgrounds. He was observing the transformation of the colors and the individual forms. Next he put aside the cheese plant that had been his model, and let his imagination guide the scissors running through the paper.

Look back at Matisse's black leaf on a red background, one leaf of his cheese plant. It is not a silhouette or a photograph of a real plant, but the personal expression of a leaf—Matisse's leaf! "One must study an object for a long time," he wrote, "to know what its sign is."

The Sheaf is a maquette, or model, that Matisse made for a ceramic mural. Now it was no longer the leaf itself that interested him, but its potential—how it could *work* as an element of a larger composition. These leaves seem to have been cast to the surface like the glittering spray from a waterfall, caught in the seconds before they scatter out to fill the entire page, the whole wall. They illuminate the paper with an explosion of life—like fireworks. Matisse felt that life was like "a growing sheaf of forces tied, and opening out in all directions." Perhaps he tried to illustrate that here. You can look at the shapes around you—clouds, shadows, smoke, or flames, for example—and invent your own signs.

The Sheaf 1953
size 294 cm x 350 cm

Painting flat colors

"To work with scissors," said Matisse, "is an occupation in which I can lose myself." Here's an opportunity for you to do so, too. You have more strength, more time and vigor than Matisse. First prepare your paper.

You will need thick, smooth tagboard, poster paints or gouache, a large, flat paintbrush, a pitcher of clean water, a clean glass jar, and sheets of newspaper to work on.

When you paint on paper, you can produce many different effects without mixing colors. The most difficult effect to achieve is a smooth surface. Here are some tricks to help.

Dip the paintbrush into the pitcher of water. Thoroughly wet one sheet of paper with the brush. Let the water soak in.

Squeeze some paint into the jar and add enough water to make a smooth, runny paste. Stir the mixture with your brush until it is like cream. Make sure you have enough paint to cover a whole sheet of paper at once.

Cutting shapes

Your paper is prepared. Now find a shape. Do as Matisse did: look around you, inside you. Take your scissors. Feel the resistance of the paper under your blades. With practice, your scissors will slide through the color, and the shape you are hunting will be free!

When your brush is soaked with paint, start stroking the color on the paper. Using a fast and regular rhythm, stroke always in the same direction, without passing over your previous strokes. Lay this sheet of paper on the newspaper to dry.

Try to vary the "intensity" of color. By using more or less water, you can make the color weaker or stronger, but the smoothness will remain.

Do you agree with Matisse that a pair of scissors is a marvelous instrument? It teaches you how to draw, to sculpture, in color. And for every shape you cut there is another! The shape itself is called the positive, and the cutaway is the negative. They are mate elements. Keep both to compose your pictures.

13

People have surely told you that blue, red, green, or yellow suits you. You may think this means that you look prettier or more striking. What really happens is that the color you are wearing against your skin brings out, or wakes up, the color of your eyes, your hair, or your cheeks. This particular color creates a harmonious atmosphere that helps you to shine.

Colors play with each other. Colors can destroy or enhance each other when they are close together. Look at the blue shapes on different-colored backgrounds and compare them with the different-colored shapes on blue. Half shut your eyes and look at each shape in turn. You will see how different in size and intensity they look. Against the light, bright colors, the outlines of the blue shapes become sharper. Against the dark backgrounds, the shapes are blurred. The color, therefore, influences the aspect of the shape and the intensity of the background.

Colors create an impression on your eyes. Stare at each of the colored shapes in turn, and concentrate. A glow of moving color and brightness will appear around each one. Now squeeze up your eyes and look at each shape again. The flickering of your eyelids creates a haze and makes the colors merge into each other.

Colors give you different sensations. They can trigger in you a flow of images, sounds, emotions. Think of blue. You might see a sky, a sea, a cornflower, and feel freshness and lightness. Think of green. You see, perhaps, fresh grass, dark pine forests, peppermint, and your mind drifts to spring. Red suggests flames, and yellow the sun.

Color can also remind you of smell, taste, or an atmosphere around you. You describe colors as warm, cold, tender, acid, and so on, because of your own experiences. So colors have become symbols: red for passion, green for hope, blue for peace, black for sorrow, white for purity.

Composition, Violet and Blue 1947
size 40.5 cm x 86 cm

Composition, the Velvets 1947
size 51.5 cm x 217.5 cm

Matisse said that everything we see passes through the eye, to be filed in a little room and then amplified by the imagination. In 1947 he was making lots of cutouts that he filed away, then used as the need arose, pairing and combining his images on rectangular sheets of paper. Both *Composition, Violet and Blue* and *Composition, the Velvets* were made at this time.

In the first of the compositions, each sheet contains one dominant image. The shapes belong to the same family, but through the use of color and texture, Matisse created a completely different sort of feeling in each. The left-hand shape is hard and precise, while the right-hand shape is soft. The left-hand image is put into focus by its dark background. The image on the right-hand sheet is less obvious because of its dappled texture against the soft background color. Starting from the background colors, work out how Matisse built his effects, and see what they evoke in you.

The colored panels of *The Velvets* are organized in a strong vertical format which has a rhythm, like the beats in a bar of music. The complete panel unfolds like a melody. See how the composition is built. Backgrounds first: warm or hot colors in the center; on the right, cold, lighter colors; on the left, dark colors. If you squeeze up your eyes tightly, the leaves will almost disappear, leaving you with a band of flowing colors. Notice how the whites come to the surface, and how the composition moves, like a long flag tossing in the wind.

Put your hands over *The Velvets* and discover each panel slowly, one after the other. Move from left to right, from right to left, or from the center. Open your hands over the large orange panel, then move them apart. Slowly the black shapes appear, and block in those warm, glowing effects. If you look at a painting in a museum, you will enjoy it more if you step back and stretch up your hand to block out parts in the same way.

Light and color

The colors of Matisse's cutouts are flat and pure. They have come straight from the paint tubes. But these colors, once on paper, are influenced by many factors.

Colors come from light. A rainbow sparkling in the sun carries drops of colored light. Light changes colors. Take your sheets of smooth, colored paper and experiment: put them in the dark, in the shade, in the sun, near a lamp or a candle. Your colors will never look the same

Light falling through color can also change it. If you put a sheet of tracing paper against the window and paint a stroke of gouache on it, the light coming through will be colored.

Texture and color

Texture also influences color. The same blue looks different on smooth, shiny paper than on rough, absorbent paper. It is the same in nature. The blue sky when you raise your head has a different effect than the sky you see reflected in a lake.

Try playing with texture and color yourself. Put down flat color (see pages 12–13) on sheets of smooth paper and vary its appearance by creating different textures. Use the ideas shown here, then look around for other textured materials.

Roll a cork over the color when it is wet or almost dry. Or try rolling a wet, painted cork over dry white or blue paper.

The simplest way to change the effect of color is to paint different grades of paper. Try smooth, shiny paper, rough, absorbent paper, or textured paper.

Squeeze up a dry sponge and dab it on the wet paint. Squeeze in different ways, dab it flat, or use a corner. Dab over the paper again when it is dry.

Stroke an old comb through the wet paint. Make straight lines, crisscrossed lines, or curves. (Don't press too hard.) Try this using thick paint.

Press a sheet of paper towel on wet color. Or crumple a sheet and dab with that. Or pleat the paper towel and press it down. Look at the effects of the folds.

You can make wonderful textures by dipping the sleeve of an old sweater into wet paint and then pressing it firmly onto dry white paper.

Put a feather into wet paint and press it onto dry white paper. Or lay a feather on the paper and lightly dab over it with a brush full of color.

Dip an old toothbrush into wet paint, then drag it across dry paper. Press it down hard so that the bristles spread. Or dab a dry brush over wet paint.

19

Oceania, the Sky 1946
size 165 cm x 380 cm

In 1946, a textile manufacturer named Zika Ascher approached Matisse to commission some mural decorations for his offices in London. He visited Matisse several months later, and was shown the finished *Oceania* designs. Matisse pinned the white forms directly onto the beige walls of his apartment in Paris. These panels, then printed on fabric, were the artist's first large-scale cutouts.

Oceania, the Sky and *Oceania, the Sea* are an expression of what Matisse remembered about the journey he made to Tahiti and the South Pacific in 1930. Matisse explained: "The memories of my voyage to Tahiti have only now returned to me, fifteen years later, in the form of obsessive images—corals, birds, jellyfish, sponges."

20

Oceania, the Sea c. 1946
size 165 cm x 380 cm

At the time, Matisse took no photographs because he feared that "those poor images" would stop his impressions from becoming deeper. He felt it was more important to drink things in than to fix them in a second. "With my eyes wide open, I absorbed everything, as a sponge absorbs liquid," he said. The enchantment of the sky and sea was so strong that he lay soaking in their beauty.

These two panels of only two colors, beige and white, plunge us immediately into a golden atmosphere of sun and sand. Everything is light and free. The white shapes floating softly across the large, open composition, like algae on the surface of a calm sea, provide a new dimension that a photograph could never give us.

Polynesia, the Sky 1946
size 200 cm x 314 cm

In these two compositions, Matisse structured the ground in a checkerboard of contrasting blues across which he pinned the white cutouts. The "signs" are similar to those in *Oceania*—corals, jellyfish, algae bordering the edges. But here the energy is stronger. Flip the pages to compare the moods of *Oceania* and *Polynesia:* openness, calm, sand, warmth in one; in the next, energy, movement, freshness, sea and wind. Matisse watched doves flying for so long that their movement glided in his head. The flapping of their wings, their curves, guided his scissors: these white birds could then fly around his cutout.

Polynesia, the Sea 1946
size 196 cm x 314 cm

Colors worked on Matisse as forces. "A certain blue enters my soul, a certain red affects my blood pressure, another color wakes me up," he said. "I don't cut the oranges and reds like the greens and blues."

Matisse saw in color and light the source of health, happiness, and life itself. He would surround the beds of sick friends with his canvases to cure them. He surrounded himself with his own cutouts. Matisse claimed throughout his life to be able to control the mood of those who saw his paintings. His friend the French poet Aragon always spoke about him as a kind of sorcerer.

Whatever Matisse's cutouts were to become—rugs, tapestries, murals, religious vestments, scarves, books, or pictures—he was confronted with a surface on which something would happen, where his colors and signs would express his feelings. He wanted to create an "art of balance" in a space, "where everything had its share...everything was expressive...where one had to preserve the beauty of each color through organization and construction." The theme of *Mimosa* comes from the festival of flowers in Nice, where massive floats drive through hot streets bordered by mimosa trees, where the drifting scent of these tiny yellow flowers fills the air.

Picture a scene of flowers yourself. Shut your eyes and think of violets, irises, daffodils, poppies, tulips. You are composing with a rainbow of petals. Now start again. This time, imagine only yellows—buttercups, daffodils, yellow daisies. Then add a poppy! The subtle harmonies of yellow are suddenly disturbed. The poppy sets the bunch on fire. Add whites, pinks, and blues to put the fire out. The balance of colors is changing all the time.

Matisse said: "An avalanche of colors has no strength. It's only when they are organized that they can express the emotion of an artist." The choice of colors is never arbitrary. Remember this when you compose pictures.

Mimosa 1949–1951
size 148 cm x 96.5 cm

25

In 1942 Matisse was asked to do an illustrated album of cutouts. This book that he first thought of as a "penny plaything" was to mark a crucial point in the last phase of his career. He called the book *Jazz,* for he often compared the rhythm of cutting paper to the spirit of jazz music.

These three *Lagoon* pictures are the last images he made for *Jazz.* They share the same title, were made simultaneously, and are based on Matisse's memories of the South Pacific.

If you look at these three pictures, you seem to be seeing things in stages. *Lagoon I* gives an overall impression, a vision from far above, far away. In *Lagoon II* and *III,* things seem to be getting closer. It is as if Matisse was first of all catching a feeling. Then, by searching in his mind and emotions, he remembered more precisely, and his focus got sharper.

If you study all three, you will see how Matisse developed such continuity, how he built his effects. The three images share the same shimmering colors. You will find that they also share many cutouts and cutaways.

The Lagoon (I) 1944, from *Jazz*
size 42.2 cm x 65.5 cm

The Lagoon (II) 1944, from *Jazz*
size 40.5 cm x 60.5 cm

The Lagoon (III) 1944, from *Jazz*
size 42.2 cm x 65.5 cm

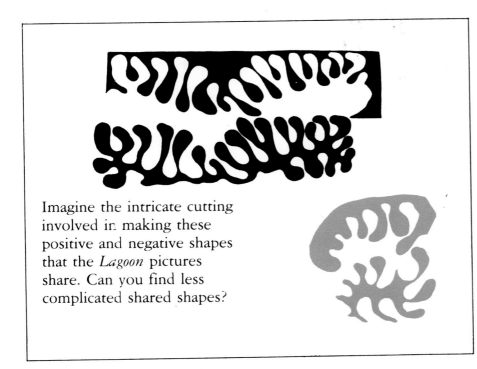

Imagine the intricate cutting involved in making these positive and negative shapes that the *Lagoon* pictures share. Can you find less complicated shared shapes?

Matisse referred to himself as a juggler—juggling with lines, forms, and colors, but also juggling with the visions in his mind. You, too, can learn the discipline of stages: of moving from dreams to ideas to careful realization.

Your eye makes the link between these cutouts, remembering the undulating lines and colors. But you have to make a conscious effort to see what fits where and to follow Matisse's process.

Look at the two examples of negative and positive shapes that the pictures share. There are many more. With tracing paper and pencil, follow the outlines in the cutouts and try to put the shapes together like a puzzle. When you come to compose your own pictures, try to cut out in one stroke so that you can use the cutaway.

Matisse wrote: "A picture is like a book. Like a book on a shelf...it needs to give up its riches...the action of the reader who must pick it up, open it, and shut himself away with it. ... In the same way, a picture cannot be penetrated unless our attention is especially concentrated on it."

27

Icarus 1943
size 40.5 cm x 27 cm

This cutout, *The Fall of Icarus*, was also made and printed for *Jazz*. Icarus, according to Greek legend, was given a pair of wax and feather wings. But the boy, being overambitious, flew too close to the sun. The wax melted, and Icarus fell to his death in the sea.

Let your eyes slide around the picture. A tiny red dot, much smaller than any other shape, makes Icarus's heart beat for you. The yellow stars flicker, and that big clumsy body lifts and soars. Everything has its place. Whether the stars look like stars, or like shells crashing through the heavens, is unimportant. The heart is too round, the legs are too short. It does not matter. Matisse is offering you *his* falling Icarus.

Of course, it is difficult to imagine the actual size of the picture by looking at a reproduction. Perhaps that is not important here because, whatever its size, you instinctively feel that the space it occupies could not be filled in a different way. The picture has perfect balance. You feel that you could throw yourself into this starred night and follow Icarus and his passion.

Matisse took great pains to explain to his students that the apparent simplicity of his work was the result of a lifetime of discipline and effort. Like Icarus, Matisse was a man of passion. He saw his art as a journey to an ideal land, and the world as a platform from which he could take off. His life was a constant search, each picture a stepping stone on a path toward beauty and perfection. At each painting, Matisse burned his wings. Patiently he would start again in his quest, and each renewed effort would celebrate his search for light and color. Always for him it was the voyage, the journey of discovery, that mattered.

The Snail 1952
size 69 cm x 89 cm

You might look at this simple cutout of a snail, turn it upside down, squeeze up your eyes, and still think that it doesn't look like a snail. Why not a question mark or a flower? Listen to Matisse: "That paper cutout, the kind of volute, that you see on the wall up there is a stylized snail. First of all I drew the snail from nature, holding it between two fingers. Drew and drew. I became aware of an unfolding. I formed in my mind a purified sign for a shell. Then I took my scissors."

Try to follow what Matisse is saying; live his creative process and learn from his experience. Pick up a snail, or a shell on a beach. Draw it from all possible angles, as shown here. Understand how it is built, find the center, the spiral. Put a flashlight to it and see the transparency of the shell: you can see many aspects of the same object— texture, color, construction. When you draw it over and over again as Matisse did, all your vision, all your energy is concentrated on that single object, and for a while it will become your whole world.

Often by fixing on one object, your vision, instead of narrowing, opens up and embraces many feelings and emotions. Here, in his own way, Matisse moved from the particular—that little snail—to the general—a spiral common to all shells; from a shape to a movement, from close observation of nature to abstraction of an idea. The observation, contemplation, and understanding had been a long, thoughtful process. The liberation of the image from the paper, then, took only a few seconds.

Try to see things in this way. Take a leaf, and draw it— first the shape, the general form of it; then forget the shape and look at how it is built, the central stem with veins leading from it. Let your memories come back. See the leaf on a branch, climb down the tree in your mind, take a few steps back, look at the tree: the general shape first, then the tree with no leaves, the hefty trunk, the branches leading from the trunk. Does the tree remind you of the way a single leaf is built? Is it a labyrinth of shapes, or something with vertical and diagonal lines? Or does it give you the idea of growth and birth? A little leaf can take you on a long journey into your own abstract world.

Looking at a shell from the front, from above, or sideways will change your feeling for it. You may even see the shell as if it were huge, like a cave.

Matisse cut out lots of different shapes of all colors and sizes, and organized this vast composition called *The Snail*. It took an enormous amount of time, calculating and readjusting, with his assistants pinning and moving the shapes around until their master's sense of balance and harmony was satisfied.

Again, you may find this a very strange snail. Why such a big picture for such a small animal? And why so many colors? Why cut out shapes with such hard corners? At least a snail is vaguely round! There is no solution to all these questions. There doesn't have to be, but there *is* an answer for each of us. Matisse isn't telling us this is what a snail looks like, or this is how *you* must show a snail. He is only giving us yet another image for our minds to enjoy. Someone once told him: "If I saw a woman like the ones you do in the street, I would run for my life." He answered: "I am not painting a woman. I am painting a picture." The same is true for *The Snail*.

The Snail might suggest a spiral around which the square shapes are built—the "unfolding" Matisse described when he spoke about doing the smaller picture of *The Snail*. But Matisse also called this picture *Chromatic Composition*. This title gives us the idea that his main interest was to organize the colors in a specific way. Notice how the colors are arranged. Each is against a white background, and each touches at least two other colors. The spiral itself is built of warm colors. The title of a picture is there to help you understand what the artist tried to show you, although you can look for other images. You may find an unfolding caterpillar or a spiral of smoke. Try to use the colors and shapes in this composition, arranging your papers in a totally different order, to create your own "Chromatic Composition."

The Snail 1952
size 286 cm x 287 cm

Woman Seated with Arm on Head
1952
size 27 cm x 21 cm

O ne must study an object for a long time," said Matisse. This composition, *Blue Nude IV*, is yet another example of the artist's painstaking creative process. He worked for a whole year developing this theme of *Blue Nudes*, although these figures are much like his early paintings and sculptures. It took a notebook of twenty-eight drawings for *Blue Nude IV*, and two weeks of cutting and arranging the cutouts before Matisse was satisfied. Only then, having patiently created the pose for one, did he proceed to do three variations.

At first, Matisse worked with small individual cutouts. He would pin or glue them to the walls, where they created an atmosphere of color and light. Soon these floating forms became living landscapes into which the artist could escape. He started drawing on the walls and ceiling from his bed. Using a long bamboo pole with a thick piece of charcoal on the end, Matisse began to create larger and larger compositions.

Matisse drawing on his walls

Blue Nude IV 1952
size 102.9 cm x 76.8 cm

The Parakeet and the Mermaid 1952
size 337 cm x 773 cm

In 1952, pink and green flowers started growing over Matisse's bedroom walls. "You see," he wrote, "as I am obliged to remain often in bed...I have made a little garden all around me where I can walk."

In this garden there are familiar signs: leaves, fruit, a
bird, a nude figure. "I had to make this parakeet with
colored paper," Matisse wrote. "Well, I became a parakeet
and found myself in the work."

During the day, Matisse's little garden was growing in his bedroom, and at night another adventure was developing in his dining room. "I have always loved the sea," he wrote, "and now that I can no longer go for a swim I have surrounded myself with it."

The garden had developed slowly, through trial and error. But Matisse had a clear vision of *The Swimming Pool* in his head from the beginning. He was impressed once by a lady swimming in an aquarium on the stage of a music hall in Paris. He might have had that in mind when he composed the picture.

His first act was to stretch a large band of heavy white paper around the entire room. The bathers, leaping in and out of the long rectangular strip, stretch out like elastic bands. Sometimes the swimmers are blue; sometimes it is the white negative shapes surrounded by color that give the bathers their form. Matisse's cutout is unlike any swimming pool you have ever seen. It is unlike any swimming pool Matisse had ever seen. It is a memory of the splashes he was too old to be able to do again.

The Swimming Pool is possibly one of Matisse's greatest achievements in the medium of the cutout. From the detailed, small-scale work he moved on to attempt one of the most complex of designs. He used the possibilities of the positive and negative shapes to create a whole world of movement, light, and energy. But what is perhaps most moving about *The Swimming Pool* is the burst of life, strength, and freedom that this old, crippled man was capable of expressing for us.

The Swimming Pool 1952
mounted on two panels
size 230 cm x 1645 cm

39

Playing with space

After seeing how Matisse proceeded, you may feel the need to wander about in a space of your own. Matisse made several cutouts for screens. You could start with this idea. If you put small models in front of the screen, all the proportions will change and that background will look like a whole wall.

Before you start, choose the mood you want to create on your screen: for instance, calm, movement, joy, anger, cold, warmth. Then choose your theme: it might be night and day, sky and earth, or fire and water.

To make a sturdy screen, you will need strong cardboard. You could use separate sheets or four sides of a box. You will also need a wet sponge and six strips of sticky brown paper tape cut to the same depth as your screen. Then collect your materials for painting (see pages 12–13). To make a picture, you will also need colored paper, scissors, map pins, and glue. "Day-night" is just one theme you could try.

Sponge the sticky side of the tape, one strip at a time. Put the strips lengthwise on one side, widthwise on the other, to hinge the panels of cardboard.

Clear your mind before you come to arrange the screen. First, put all your warm colors—the reds, oranges, and yellows—together. Put cold ones together, too. Then pin them up one by one on the panels of the screen. Keep moving them about until you are pleased with the result. Then glue each one in turn in its final position.

Paint both sides of the panels smoothly (see pages 12–13). Let this dry. Work in the opposite direction to add a second coat of paint.

Draw a pattern for your shapes or cut them straight from your sheets of colored paper. You could cut through two or three sheets together if

you need lots of the same shape. Or fold the paper and cut through all the folds for a different effect.

Wall frieze

If you ask your parents first, you could make a picture go right around your room. Look at the room to see how the light falls on the walls. Cut lengths of nonadhesive shelf paper and pin it vertically or horizontally, depending on the space you want to use. Then arrange your cutouts on it and proceed as you did for the screen.

At the end of his life, Matisse wrote that his only religion was the love for the work he had to do, his love for creation and true sincerity. From 1948 to 1952 he devoted most of his energy to one single project—the Chapel of the Dominicans at Vence. "I created this chapel with the desire only to express myself totally with shape and color."

Matisse saw the chapel as a whole and created every detail for it: the space, the roof, walls and ceramics, the stained glass windows, the altar, crucifix, candlesticks. For the priests, he designed vestments in glowing colors, like the Rose Chasuble.

Matisse used colored stained glass and black-and-white ceramics to balance the black-and-white habits of the nuns with the brighter colors of the vestments of the priests, "as if there were four voices singing in the chapel: two in color, two in black and white."

Rose Chasuble 1950–1952
size 130 cm x 200 cm

The Tree of Life (nave) 1949
size 515 cm x 515 cm

The cutout here is the maquette, or model, for one of the three chapel windows. Matisse said it was like the musical notation for a symphony: it indicates only the colors, shapes, and size, just as written music shows you the notes and how the music is played, but is not yet sound. The symphony swells to reality only when the light has passed through the stained glass.

The light streaming through the windows makes the colors vibrate and come alive. Originally, stained glass windows provided only colored light, geometrical patterns through which the light played on the walls and on the floors, as in the windows of Chartres Cathedral or the temples of the East. Later, the windows were used to tell stories of the church or the saints. The windows became more decorative, but the play of light was lost.

Matisse wanted to return to the original concept "that the stained glass window is an orchestra of light." Violins, trumpets, cellos produce different tones. Each note vibrates differently. Suddenly the orchestra begins to play—instruments and notes do not exist anymore as such. The melody, the tune, all the emotion and feeling, become a whole and take over. In the same way, each color in the window is separate, but the light streaming through the colors envelops us like a symphony. Matisse explained that he could not introduce red into the chapel. However, the blue, green, and yellow glass combine to create a warm glow, which may vary from pink to violet. "I wanted a church full of gaiety," Matisse said, "so that those who come to visit will leave it happy and rested."

In this chapel, Matisse called on all his knowledge, wisdom, and love to express the light he had inside him. Whenever you pick up a pencil, a paintbrush, or scissors, open your heart and remember Henri Matisse's words: "One must observe a lot. One has only one life, and one is never finished."

The interior of the Chapel at Vence showing the *Tree of Life* windows in the nave and in the apse